The Secret Science of the Soul: How to Transcend Common Sense and Get What You Really Want From Life

Dan Desmarques

Published by 22 Lions Bookstore, 2020.

Table of Contents

Copyright Page 1

About the Publisher 3

Introduction 5

Chapter 1: Why Resentment Traps Your Thoughts? 7

Chapter 2: Why You Must Ignore the Need for Acceptance? 9

Chapter 3: Why You Must Prioritize Reason Over Love? 13

Chapter 4: Why You Must Focus on What is Important? 15

Chapter 5: Which Topics You Shouldn't Discuss? 19

Chapter 6: How to Choose Wisely? 21

Chapter 7: How to Help Yourself by Helping Others? 25

Chapter 8: How to Find Eternal Bliss? 29

Chapter 9: How to Empower Your Mind? 31

Chapter 10: How to Balance Truth and Desire? 33

Chapter 11: How to Attract the Lifestyle You Want? 37

Chapter 12: Why You Shouldn't Confuse God with Religion? 39

Chapter 13: How to Overcome Your Psychological Weaknesses? 43

Chapter 14: Why You Must Prioritize Self-Respect Over Love? 45

Chapter 15: The 7 Levels of Consciousness 49

Chapter 16: How to Identify the Rotten Apples of Society? 51

Chapter 17: What to Expect From the Higher Stages of Consciousness? 55

Chapter 18: How to Identify Truthful Knowledge? 59

Chapter 19: Why is Society Disintegrating by Default?..........................63

Chapter 20: Why You Are What You Do?..67

Chapter 21: Where Does Wisdom Come From?....................................69

Chapter 22: Why are Narcissists Our Greatest Teachers?........................73

Chapter 23: What is the Correlation Between Reincarnation and Mental Health?..77

Chapter 24: What the Personality is from a Spiritual Viewpoint?...........81

Copyright Page

The Secret Science of the Soul: How to Transcend Common Sense and Get What You Really Want From Life

By Dan Desmarques

Copyright © Dan Desmarques, 2020 (1st Ed.). All Rights Reserved.

Published by 22 Publishing

About the Publisher

About the 22 Lions Bookstore:

www.22Lions.com

Facebook.com/22Lions

Twitter.com/22lionsbookshop

Instagram.com/22lionsbookshop

Pinterest.com/22lionsbookshop

Introduction

In this generation-defining good and bad, many authors and speakers, disguised as role-models and superstar pioneers of the new world, come forth to supposedly enlighten crowds and attract followers, while promising that they can lead everyone to the much sought answers.

Such seductive approach has been very appealing to the masses, that now live in a complete darkness about their fate and purpose as human beings. And yet, simultaneously, many also eventually realize that something is wrong with the help being offered and the many gurus that appear enlightened. And so, they continue on this search, unsatisfied with the wisdom received.

This, until they find someone that has been in many religious groups, has a scientific approach to all, is experienced in explaining the a complex approach to live in simple terms, and is not afraid to talk about the truth, while also exposing it from his own viewpoint and with plenty of life experience supporting such insights. He does not talk about being positive or happy without showing exactly what these terms mean and how they can be seen. And this honest truth is what truly enlightens a civilization.

The world needs leaders more than it needs saviors. And this book will show you exactly how to become the leader you wish you had in your life.

The book also shows a new but complete approach to life, including the wisdom of the oldest generations on earth, while also unveiling the path of the future towards which the most enlightened among us are already heading. And it doesn't promise you anything, but instead shows you the raw reality around you, and how this physical universe is, despite what many want, guided by spiritual rules.

It is not a book of theories but rather an empirical guide to live than you can apply just by looking at your own existence.

In seeing such divine laws, you will be able to gain more courage, faith and belief in your true self, which will then reinforce your capacity to reach your goals in life.

Chapter 1: Why Resentment Traps Your Thoughts?

Any argument that reinforces itself without allowing a rise of consciousness, is a struggle for the predominance of the ego and not a search for the truth or a real understanding among individuals. And, the ego emerges out of the need for social ascension, the ambition for power, recognition and validation. Therefore, you can't be at your best if you are always explaining yourself to someone.

On both sides of society, either it is religion or some evil character trying to persuade you to quit your dreams, they will engage in a confrontation for your rights, forcing you to explain yourself, to basically, waste your time for long enough for you to fail.

Time is the most important asset on earth. Life is short. And even shorter when you are working towards your goals. And even shorter than that, if such goals contradict the interests of the many and their status quo.

Expect the greater opposition to the greatest impact, on any side of society. The man who is winning and changing the world, will have but few friends, and enemies everywhere.

This isn't just theory. As an author, I have been insulted by dozens of religious members, but also atheists, psychopaths and even the women who shared a house with me. The more important my work became, the more aggressive and vast my opposition became.

That, however, wasn't where it all started. As a student, I was constantly being insulted by my teachers too. Because I was already overthinking them. They had to stop me before I could do something drastic with my abilities, i.e., turn into an author.

None of them told me I should be one. But they did said, and often, that my writing style is confusing and uninteresting. And it was in their insults that I found the cause of their jealousy.

If it wasn't for their strong hatred towards my thinking and writing potential, I would never know that I should be a writer.

Should I thank them? Hell, no! I hope they all day miserably, with much pain, and then reincarnate as pigs, and get slaughtered miserably with kicks on their head.

Those demons deserve no mercy.

However, as you can see, they didn't stop me. On the contrary, I care little about what people think of what I write. I have published too many books to care.

My purpose is to elevate mankind, even if the vast majority is too stupid to see it.

I don't allow myself to get distracted any longer.

Chapter 2: Why You Must Ignore the Need for Acceptance?

The more one depends on social validation, the less likely he or she is to act in a spiritual way. And so, as you can see, any form of social media promotes anti-spiritual behaviors, more than anti-social.

The habit of using social media, for whatever purpose it is, disintegrates your mind, by controlling your attention to a huge variety of topics that are everything but related to the discovery of your true self.

Another problem with social media is that it makes us more vulnerable to social opinion, by exposing our personal interests and curiosities.

Privacy became a word of the past. Now, overall exposure is the norm. Women are proud to post naked photos of themselves, and talk about the music they like and why. People don't have shame or concerns about their identity, and then accept the fear of discrimination as the norm.

They are voluntarily alienating themselves.

On the other hand, whenever you have a personality, you will necessarily face opposition. And it's when we allow ourselves to become egotistically hurt, that resentment takes over our consciousness.

That's when the mind becomes blocked to self-awareness. We then become paranoid about changing the outcome of what has already occurred.

This is particularly common when we are victims of narcissistic abuse, as due to their own low nature, tend to bring other people down by attacking their own ego — what is exposed the most.

Once we allow ourselves to succumb to resentment, we succumb to depression, anxiety and nervousness, the greatest enemies of the mind.

In fact, social media has allowed some people to murder others at the distance, simply by abusing them psychologically for long enough.

At the very least, when you are worried about what someone is saying about you, you lose your focus, and then gain a higher predisposition for accidents.

Resentment also imprisons the mind in the past, denies our present and steals our future. One needs greater ambitions and self-love in order to overcome this state. And as we can see every day, love is not as abundant as it should be in this world.

Most people are too preoccupied with themselves, and their needs, and their obsessions.

Mediation does help in controlling the mind, and in doing so, take charge of our emotions. But you can't suppress reality, without paying a heavy price for it, in the form of a lack of capacity to make decisions wisely.

Those who go through life by abusing different substances are numbing themselves, and not truly confronting their problems.

You need to feel anger to confront your problems, because anger is the emotions everyone escapes from when numbing themselves with various substances.

Somehow, somewhere, someone told them that being angry was bad, and then they went into this confusion, of being injustice and not being able to express their emotions.

The real attack of a narcissist, for example, isn't as much directed at infuriating the victim, as it is at numbing down such individual. Because, in order to escape the emotions, the victim has to suppress the normal analytical reaction to the abuse. And in doing so, inevitably, the victim predisposes itself to more abuse.

At one point, it doesn't matter what anyone else says, because the victim of narcissistic abuse considers such abuse justifiable.

That's when the narcissist wins, when the victim has been so abused that she or he, now, instead of reacting, simply justifies the abuse in his or her own head.

Many governments use the same tactics to control the population. In China, for example, people are so traumatized with violations to their privacy, that they stop caring about it. And it's at that point, that they simply start acting as if they had none. In other words, they don't even dare talking about the government in their own house.

At that point, the government owns their soul.

That's why talking to a Chinese about Communism often causes cognitive dissonance, and they react aggressively to it, as if their life was being threatened. They behave exactly as victims of narcissistic abuse. And they are willing to die for their abusers too. And maybe they should. Maybe that's the only way to end their own tyranny.

Chapter 3: Why You Must Prioritize Reason Over Love?

The victims of narcissists are rarely able to escape their own emotions, unless they overcome them by the act of constant meditation and mental self-programming.

That's like walking ten steps forward and ten steps backwards every day. You become too busy with your own sanity to do anything else in life.

Another option, is to simply leave the oppressive environment. And I have seen many dramatic changes in people who simply removed themselves from one situation to spend a month or two somewhere else, in another country.

Quite often, that's enough for them to realize their own situation.

Mediation, on the other hand, doesn't deny this potential awareness, but rather, if well done, prepares us for it.

Contrary to popular belief, meditation has more to do with preparing the mind for confrontation than succumbing to it.

The greatest theorists on mediation were warriors, not peasants.

Meditation can also be compared to looking down on life from a higher and wider approach, as if we were flying above the Earth

That is why traveling can have a healing effect. It disconnects us from an environment and allows us to recharge our energies for a better approach to it.

From that angle of observation we are able to place reason above love, which allows us to view empathy at various levels, among which there is narcissistic love. Because they can indeed feel love, even thought their love is actually a strong form of attraction rooted on need for validation.

As one of my former narcissistic girlfriends used to say: "I love you because you take care of me, you take me to other countries, you cook for me, and you protect me."

In resume, me, me, me, me, or simply, me.

The word love has been so misused by many throughout history, that it behooves us to take it as a symbol of your humanity, which is broken, and as much as our conceptualization of love.

Humanity starts in the family and we have seen how deteriorating they are in today's world. Whenever families are breaking apart, and people are falling out of love within the group that should protect them and educate them well, society doesn't stand much of a chance.

The parallels between promiscuity and violence among children raised in a single parent home is a testament to this fact. And the fact that just saying this creates such an outrage in many, is a testimony to their own lack of capacity to introspect beyond what they were told to believe.

Few are able to think for themselves. Few are capable of seeing how they have been deceived with implanted values. And fewer, are capable of facing segregation when moving apart from the lies many still believe in. As a matter of fact, I've noticed that many men believe in whatsoever their wife tells them to believe, simply because they are afraid to disagree with her. And in what does her wife believes? In what her friends believe.

It has never been so easy to control billions of people as now. But we are still far from the extraordinary accomplishments that having microchips implanted in the body could allow.

For now, the greatest propaganda machine comes in the form of movies, who use the most common emotions, such as love, to implant abnormal values in the masses.

Chapter 4: Why You Must Focus on What is Important?

Without a purpose external to us, there is hardly any reason to motivate self-knowledge and an understanding of life. For the masses, the basic needs of every day life are the only thing they have to keep them from completely derailing psychologically.

This doesn't mean that people are willing to improve themselves when forced. Most won't but rather protest any attempt in that direction.

However, it is important to distinguish here responsibility from guilt, as there is a difference between having to go through life improving oneself or simply not contributing to society in any way.

You see, whatsoever is the political side of anyone, all agree that we must contribute to the collective well-being. Even those who profit from the masses, understand that they couldn't without their agreement. That's why psychiatry is constantly inventing names of mental illnesses to justify selling drugs that were invented before those same diseases were supposedly found.

Responsibly is then evident as the need to correct something this harming someone else or ourselves.

On the other hand, we never betray society as much as we can betray ourselves. We can't possibly be good enough when the values we defend are self-degrading, as when the Chinese join the communist party thinking that they are contributing for their country in doing so, and allowing themselves to be indoctrinated furthermore.

As a matter of fact, one of the most interesting things about human beings, is that, no matter how much and how well they justify their behaviors and actions, the same people never forgive when others do the same to them, if the behavior if indeed destructive.

That's why the greatest fear of communism is communism itself. That's why many communist leaders, once achieving power, make sure they can murder as many of those who helped them get there.

This topic leads us to the importance of accepting accountability.

It is a human quality that allows the correction of our dynamics as a society.

This, however, requires a greater understanding of the system of cause and effect within the world.

When people, inside a company, for example, compete against one another, for promotions, reputation and validation, among their coworkers, they forget that they are a team, and that the effects are outside of the team, in the goals that the company wants to fulfill. It is then no wonder that, when the Department of Human Resources decides to investigate the causes of low performance and absence from work, it comes to the conclusion that there is a need for an investment on courses that teach how to do meditation, breathe and learn self-love.

It may sound ridiculous from a business perspective, to see that adding plants to the office, teaching workers about self-love, allowing people to listen to music while they work, and offering them cakes and fruits, has a tremendous impact on productivity. And few question why it really works.

The reason why, is this: people don't understand the effects of their productivity, they don't see themselves there, and quite often, they don't care either.

Most people are so detached from reality that they can't even see the causation of whatever they do or say to others.

It would be funny if we were talking about children and not adults.

The only time I saw this spiritual principle being implemented, was in India. A business owner decided to share the results with his workers every month, and increase their salary accordingly.

He also used to pin a bunch of motivational quotes on the wall at the entrance. And as you can imagine, not only did he save a lot of money on motivational courses, but also increased the motivation and earnings of his own employees at the same time.

When I met him, he asked me many questions about his business strategy, and all I could do was praise him and guide him towards my most recent books. Many years later, we still keep in contact, which allowed me to confirm that his company was awarded recently by the Minister of Commerce in India.

You see, he doesn't just motivate the employees, but also pulls them towards a higher conscientiousness and level of responsibility, and that has a significant impact on his workers and even on his business, which invariably is noticed by the country itself.

Chapter 5: Which Topics You Shouldn't Discuss?

There is nothing that a narcissist will oppose so strongly as self-development. Quite often, by using ridicule and plausible doubt.

As soon as you start focusing on your dreams, the concept of team work, the need for compromise and commitment or empathy, that's when the garbage comes to the surface, and manifests itself.

Defense attorneys, indeed, have much to learn from narcissists, as they hold the best techniques of mass manipulation.

It is very difficult to detect who is stopping you from reaching your goals, when you are not aware of the techniques used against you, most of which, are disguised as care and help.

Purpose, willingness and responsibility, lead to consciousness, and are opposed precisely by those who oppose consciousness the most — the broken, resentful, and evil. And that's a large portion of society.

Responsibility, being a precursor of thought, can only be gained with the consciousness that comes from the soul, in the awakening of itself for the truth. And that requires, at first, introspection, and the ability to confront our own limitations and sufferings.

The first spiritual sacrifice one makes in this journey is actually the sacrifice of himself - his ego and pride. And it is difficult to do that if others are pushing you to protect such ego, by attacking your pride on chasing a new path. Because pride is relative but ego is not.

Suffering does purifies but only when it is the consequence of a higher purpose. And defending your rights to society is not.

In fact, you only understand happiness when you stop feeling the need to justify yourself.

We can't fully understand the importance of happiness, without first feeling the effects of suffering the lack of it. Because we can naturally be happy, but as soon a consciousness interrupts our development, this happiness becomes codependent of our maturity as a spiritual being.

That's why we can't blame children of a lack of awareness as it is not innate to their biological capacities, but we can certainly judge any adult for not being conscientious enough.

This fact can be seen from wider angles, as we attract that what we wish to focus our attention on.

We are not victims of reality but co-creators, and how we deal with what comes in our direction is far more important than what really happens.

Chapter 6: How to Choose Wisely?

Quite often, because we cannot see all the elements forming the reality around us and the experiences coming in our direction, we focus on what we observe and how we feel, rather than what is occurring from a spiritual perspective.

We then become an effect of that reality, rather than co-creators, capable of changing the results in our life.

Let us consider, for example, the case of a woman who is afraid of falling in love.

Imagine that this woman meets a man who considers her to be charismatic and attractive. Although her good fortune finds her, she rejects it, in order to withdraw back to the cycle of pain she is familiar with. But we determine our future with every decision made in the present, therefore, it is the decision, and not our past, that affects the future the most.

We only have the illusion that the past determines our future, because we allow our emotions to control our decisions.

The totality of the network representing the virtual sketch of our reality is built out of many decisions in time. Each intersecting line, leading from one point into another, is created with a decision. Therefore, even though we are not in control of our destiny, we are in full control of how such destiny looks like. Coincidentally, that is also how our thoughts, memory and identity develop.

We can then easily conclude that moral behavior, rooted on a higher or divine perspective on life, is truthful, grants us greater wisdom, effectiveness and success. It is actually the main secret of many esoteric groups that have kept themselves underground, namely, The Pythagoreans.

The Pythagoreans dedicated themselves to studying these divine laws, in order to elevate themselves spiritually and intellectually. Many great advancements in art, mathematics, engineering and philosophy were possible due to their efforts. Even Alexander the Great, can attribute his success, and to a great extent, to the work of the Pythagoreans.

The Freemasons and the Rosicrucians are merely a glimpse in time of everything that this spiritual and intellectual school represented.

Another field in which the Pythagoreans naturally immersed themselves in studies, was fortunetelling. Because as soon as you start understanding the patterns of life, and the effects of your personal decisions in time, you are also able to easily predict outcomes with a great certainty.

That allows us to adjust our behavior accordingly and before a certain result appears, in order to shift destiny in accordance to our desires.

This is what affirmations and mind programming do. When we repeat what we wish to obtain in a daily basis, our mind starts reorganizing itself in order to make the right computations in that direction.

Visualization and the channeling of emotions towards the visions we have of what we wish to obtain, reinforce those patterns.

Everything else depends on how we act towards what is offered to us.

Many people fail, not because they lack opportunities for success, but because they don't make the decisions that lead them there. They don't trust themselves enough to acquire what they want the most. And so, they dream about their goals, attract the opportunities, and then keep blocking the manifestations. This, until they stop dreaming.

The inability to dream and cowardice are related. Many times, one needs to relearn to believe in himself before he can dream.

Those who do not trust themselves enough to make the right decisions, often fail by default, by focusing on the expectation of failure and acting accordingly.

For example, if a person expects to be abandoned, she will act as if she didn't care about being abandoned, in order to protect herself emotionally, and in doing so, she ends up being abandoned.

This is called a self-fulfilling prophecy. But this term has been so overused that the vast majority of the morons on the planet, now uses it to justify their stupidity, as when people say that it's a self-fulfilling prophecy that you detect a problem before it occurred and it occurred because you detected it.

It always amazes me how the masses take any theory, shift its meaning and then use it to justify the same: their own ignorance.

Chapter 7: How to Help Yourself by Helping Others?

Humans may be imperfect, but the dynamics of reality are not. Our perfection is shown is our actions and decisions. And those can be perfect in themselves, and despite any outcome.

For our decisions to lead us towards such maximization of perfection, we must look at the ideal outcome from a divine perspective, more than we look at our own personal desires. In other words, if you want a billion dollars, you should also keep in mind who you want to serve after having such amount of money, and which positive actions you will take with that money that will benefit the greatest amount of people.

The more altruistic a desire is, the more likely one is to get it too. The vast majority of the people can't get what they want because they are selfish in nature.

Naturally, it is very hard to be altruistic when you are suffering and in need, but that is why faith compensates for the imbalance in our reality.

The more we lack, the greater the amount of faith we need, because, certainly, the shift will have to match that faith more than our potential or possibilities.

You don't need much faith when you have abundance. It is when you don't have anything or anyone to help you that you need it the most.

When a religion welcomes the poor and the suffering but fails in teaching teach them this basic principle, it does a great disservice to them. In that case, not helping them would be best, as help with pity rather than compassion and empathy, prolongs the suffering of those in need.

As we gain consciousness through the application of moral principles and compassion, the divine order of this world becomes clearer, but this doesn't mean, however, that we will be able to adapt to this world in a permanent transformation. What we adapt to is a world that permeates the virtual structure of the physical reality, and yet, never changes.

Such world can only be seen through our highest virtues.

You may then wonder: how can the physical world change if the spiritual world remains the same?

This is a question that have led many to suspect and discredit religion. But you see, the spiritual world is made of energy, laws and codes, and those can be adapted to any situation. The future of planet earth is as related to our past as our present is. We are all evolving within the same energy, laws and codes.

This doesn't meant that the truth depends on perspective or is relative to it, but rather that this truth depends on moral laws and compassion to make sense as such. It exists beyond our personal will, and does not depend on our beliefs over time.

In fact, quantum physicists go further, to say that nothing is lost because in every decision two realities are created — for what we see and what we reject.

This could lead us to accept that, somewhere, in a parallel reality, there's another one of us that didn't make our mistakes and is living another life. And this is true, but only to a certain extent. Our consciousness dictates what is real, even though we can indeed shift and transition between many possibilities.

We do this through the use of imagination and the development of emotional attachments — in this case, the vivid imagination of a dream, and the empathizing towards the other one of us living that dream.

The right word for this is actually admiration. So then we must ask: could you be jealous of yourself? Could you hate yourself?

If you can't, or shouldn't, because it makes no sense, why hate or be jealous of others?

The physical world is merely the playground where you develop all the potentialities of your mind. If you can be kind to others, you can certainly appreciate more what God can offer you. If you can love yourself, you will certainly not be afraid to receive miracles. Everything is connected, to our heart, beliefs and attitudes.

The key to access this multidimensional portal is in the spirit, behind the veil of consciousness. And consciousness is merely the path to get there. We live the path by our virtues.

The more we can raise our awareness in what regards the dynamic between mind and spirit, and see the invisible through the visible, as well as understand the invisible through the visible, the easier it will be to forgive ourselves and others, and transcend our human nature, as well as the nature of others, to acquire powers that seem unnatural to many.

Someone who lives this way will hardly regret anything in the past, as he will also have the necessary capacity to transform the future.

We can actually say that the boundaries presented by reality are proportional to the capacity of the individual to create a new one, with new limits and challenges to entertain himself.

Chapter 8: How to Find Eternal Bliss?

Chasing goals in the physical world rarely brings anyone happiness. This is why people move in circles in life, always chasing different things, while always being unhappy, and finding it difficult to change the core of their existence.

The key to happiness lies within, in our emotions, and in building or creating a reality that balances such emotions.

The foundations of that are found in what we love to do, in being surrounded by the right people and in living in a culture we are proud of. In other words, happiness is the freedom to choose, and not to have or accept. And maybe you need to choose many times, many different things, and be wrong often, but that's how your progress externally towards your internal world.

Having, as in the form of success, is just a natural consequence of the choices made and the lessons learned.

Since social media became more intrusive in people's life, the levels of unhappiness decreased, because now, instead of focusing on material things, people are actually looking at virtual achievements, such as attention, validation and distractions. Their decisions are made from what they observe rather than who they are, even if what they observe is clearly a show shared by everyone, trying to desperately hide their difficulties in life.

People now have an anxiety for validation because social media levels that need upwards.

The need for social acceptance is one of the most important causes for the deviation of the spiritual path, not because we need to isolate ourselves to be spiritual, but because we only feel the need to be socially accepted when we are trying to associate ourselves with people who are narcissistic rather than spiritual, and social media does promote narcissism.

A real spiritual person accepts the differences in others and praises them as gifts of God or spiritual challenges to overcome. But the more someone focuses on things that will, to a great extent, not be maintained in time, such as the need for acceptance, the emptier someone will be.

As a matter of fact, the number of people that show narcissistic behaviors is quickly increasing for the same reasons. The sense of self, to a great extent, has vanished. People simply don't have the time to consider who they are because they are too busy trying to understand what others expect them to be.

It can take many years before one realizes that the material needs alone can't find a limit or a positive outcome as a valuable asset.

This is mentioned by many billionaires too, when they talk about the importance of having two bank accounts: A financial bank account and an emotional bank account. The two are interrelated.

Unless, whatsoever we are doing, leads us towards unveiling our gifts, conquer our dreams, and reveal more of our true identity, we are definitely heading for disaster, no matter what we hear from others or what it seems in present time.

That is why, whenever someone asks me for an advice on life, I always say: "Whatever you do, choose love first."

Now, the idea of love may be abstract, but everyone knows what matters the most, and that's what I am addressing here: focus on what is of the highest emotional importance to you.

Chapter 9: How to Empower Your Mind?

In order for own consciousness to manifest without any obstructions, we need to dismantle the illusory pillars that compose our idea of reality, i.e., our most deceptive values, and this isn't possible without this reality being lived and experienced first, and then effectively analyzed.

Similarly, whenever we find new satisfactions in life, we understand more about our spiritual identity, we understand better about what we really need and don't need, and above all, we understand who we truly are.

We then make decisions accordingly, to maintain pleasure and avoid pain. And that constitutes the renewed values that lead us to predictable and related outcomes.

The structure of our new reality is then formed from our system of values, and the interpretation we make of the events that occur will always be interrelated with our belief system. We won't question such events as much as we will or should question ourselves.

For example, it is not as important that someone betrays you, as it is to understand why you have chosen to have and keep such person in your life.

It is not as important why you are poor as it is to look at the reasons why you are not rich.

It is not as important that you fail in life, as it is to look at the reasons stopping you from being successful.

The odds may not be in your favor in many situations, but the odds are not there to prove you wrong either or to help you justify your failures. They are merely there to show you the full spectrum of your world.

If I used the odds to make decisions, I would certainly never have become a writer or a musician. Those are not two areas where you can succeed with the odds. But I did use them to qualify myself, and I determined that I was persistent enough and qualified to win, if I really worked hard. And that's what I did; I simply accepted whatsoever I had to do to reach my goals.

Not many people will produce 33 music albums and over 300 books, but I was willing to pay that price of production to get the benefits — turn that into my full-time occupation.

If my purpose was merely to write and produce music, then I would achieve such goal without having the freedom and wealth to justify it.

Surely, you can do whatever you want in your spare time, but it's very difficult when you are tired after a full day of work, and you have a family to raise, and especially, as you grow older and you see your level of vital energy decreasing.

You are that which you create, but what you create also change us. Therefore, indeed, "all that we are is a result of what we have thought, the mind is everything and what we think we become" (Buddha), but the mind also shapes into that which you want it to be. Your thoughts in a distant future won't be the same thoughts of your distant past, if you keep changing yourself towards your ideal self.

Chapter 10: How to Balance Truth and Desire?

We cannot pretend to be someone we are not. Not for too long, at least, and with severe consequences. What we should always do, is shift our perspective on reality, and learn to appreciate other views of it, in order to change our identity and then change our outcome. That's how our desires are kept aligned with our spirit.

This is the reason why, whenever someone asks me about the best strategy to achieve success, I always mention location.

Where you are can determine your potential. And that's the best definition of luck: being in the flow that improves your odds for success.

Few people realize that they can choose to be where they want and then shift the value of such potential.

One of the most astonishing proves of the imbecility of the masses is shown to me when almost everyone I encounter asks me this question: "Are you in this country because of work?"

Any answer that ignores reasons beyond the self, is not comprehended by the vast majority. And my answer is probably the most mysterious for the vast crowd of imbeciles: "I am where I want to be and for as long as I want".

People don't understand this concept of freedom. They think they are free, but they are mentally enslaved, and don't even know it. They can't even see it.

This leads us to ask ourselves the following: Why would so many people, who are braindead, mentally enslaves, and retarded to a great extent, want to get more from life? What moves them upwards if they don't see reasons beyond their own ego?

Well, that's the point. Most people are moved only by their ego. It's the "I want" that moves them. Just like when they tell me "I want to write a book but don't know about what".

In other words, they have nothing to say, they rarely read, they are not interested in helping anyone, they don't care about the world, and they want to write books, and expect me to somehow teach them how to do this, as if I was inventing what is in my books.

They are so stupid, that they can't even see how they insult me with their dumb questions.

This is a very personal example, but I can give you a more general one. I have come to the realization that most people don't know how to write properly. Quite a lot of the words used on search engines are not properly spelled, and they appear as the most searched words, because the majority is writing them wrongly.

Now, how can such people find the information they want, unless some expert on the topic mysteriously wrote the title of his essay or book wrongly?

No wonder books with the words "fuck" sell so much. It's one of the most common words, and only has four letters. It would be a mystery if the dumb masses couldn't even spell this one properly. And so, we end up seeing, an increasing trend of books with titles that match the idiotic masses selling more than those who possess titles that the vast majority can't understand.

Very often, what people seek is in front of their eyes already, but they can't see it, because they don't know the meaning of the word, or don't know how to write it, or don't bother to find the meaning on a dictionary.

The same applies to the people we meet. Most people ask me dumb questions, therefore, they can't understand my answers. Their questions are stupid, based on lack of knowledge, and my answers are accurate and based on experience. So what ends up happening is that it seems that my answers don't match their questions, and they either think I don't want to answer them, or they simply don't understand anything I say.

Now, don't assume that I am referring to uneducated people. The most recent examples included people with majors in philosophy, psychology and even medicine.

Stupidity is truly universal, and not segregated to those who lack formal education.

Quite often, the most wise people I met, did not possess college degrees. I met many of them in India. So I have to assume that humbleness and spirituality do enlighten people towards asking the right questions and putting the efforts to understand the answers.

Intelligence is clearly not something that the educational system promotes. Quite often, it turns people into arrogant morons. I know that because I have seen it, as a college professor.

Chapter 11: How to Attract the Lifestyle You Want?

We always attract what we want, but because what we want presents itself first hidden in the structures of reality, and may be difficult to identify and discover, we usually miss what is appearing before us, simply because we don't know how to identify it.

That identification, as mentioned previously, demands humbleness first.

Then, one must be wise enough to take what is given and know where to go, and how.

In other words, someone who has nothing to say, shouldn't write books. And if having a book is so important for a person, either to reinforce a broken ego, or get validation from others, then this person must elevate himself to his goal, by acquiring the knowledge he needs.

Just consider the goal of traveling to a certain country. You may never meet the pilot of your plane, you may have no idea of how to guide yourself inside the airports of foreign countries, and you may not even speak the language of the country where you will be, or know if you will be able to find anyone who can speak English with you, or any other language you can speak, and yet, you still have faith that you will reach your destination, and you still take the actions to get there, which, quite often include nothing more than packing your bags and buying a ticket.

Well, life works exactly in the same way, for love, jobs, and the acquisition of vast amounts of wealth. You don't know how a stranger you are attracted to will respond when you decide that you want to try to start a conversation with that person. You don't know how a business that you begun will work after a few years. You don't know how long your marriage will last. You don't know if your children will live beyond your own life, or if you will burry them before your time ends. All of these things come from faith and humbleness, and they are better experienced through faith in the outcome.

Nonetheless, most people place a huge importance on their house, job and family, and forget everything else, because it is easier for them to take care of things in their immediate surroundings, than it is to project their ambitions into a less predictable future.

To dream is easy but to chase your dreams is challenging.

The opposite of faith is doubt, and it's with doubt that the barriers of challenges we face in life stand. The more we doubt our abilities, the greater the challenges.

Most of what people consider normal, has only been made normal by their lifestyle and beliefs.

Chapter 12: Why You Shouldn't Confuse God with Religion?

Those who oppose our progress the most, will often use doubt to stop us; they will make us doubt our potential, capacities, and values. And sadly, many of such people that I have met, are inside religious groups that they promote as being rightful.

Among the many groups I have met, the worse is certainly the Jehovah Witnesses. And the reason why I mention it, is because I have seen too many spiritually devastating behaviors, devilish insults and atrocities in this group. Too much and too often not to say their name.

They are really evil. And they also represent what spiritual weakness, arrogance and stupidity can do to human beings when combined in a single congregation. Their lack of empathy and overall ruthlessness is, at the very least, shocking to experience.

One may be locked in a mental war whenever facing this duality in his life, and not knowing if he should pursue a spiritual path or a non-spiritual path. And that is why I must tell you that you can have both, while neglecting a group in particular.

I cannot say, for example, that I have seen anything wrong with the bible of any christian group I encountered. And that is the part that confuses such groups. I do believe in Jesus, the Bible and their own values. I just don't believe in them as a people. And I can prove why, and so well, that they get scared and vanish, because they are unable to debate it and confront their immoral actions. That behavior could make them reflect on their evilness, and they wouldn't be able to handle it.

There are many people who, like narcissists, are so evil, that they can't admit they are evil anymore.

Such individuals are unable to confront their own lack of integrity. That's why I talk here about their hypocrisy. Because it is important to call these groups for what they are, to protect our own spiritual values as a society.

I respect christianity but I think the Jehovah Witnesses represent a very dangerous mind control cult. At least, right now. I cannot say that they will be like this after twenty years have passed, if they are still around, or that they were like this fifty years ago.

However, it's a fact that the groups that last longer tend to survive the changes in the world because they use very vicious control techniques on their members to keep them there, mentally enslaved.

Rarely does a group survive the challenges of history based on their virtues. The most virtuous are often the first to succumb the pressures of war and persecution.

Another thing that stops people from changing is their memories of past experiences, as if the past was constantly repeating itself in the present, like a time loop. It's not, but if they see things that way, they will certainly create that loop themselves. You see, for many religious people, their obsession over the bible, make them want to recreate it in their lives, and embrace wars as a destiny that can't be avoided.

If the bible mentioned that in the last days christians would be eating horse shit, they would, just feel virtuous.

I see this pattern in many conversations I have with people. They tend to assume things about me and make questions that, rather than guide them towards knowing more about me, actually leads them to their own preconceptions and stereotypes, often reinforcing them. Because people always imagine more when they can't get the answers they want, as if a lack of answers justified a deeper amount of imbecility.

One of the questions that people ask me often is: "What is your purpose with that topic?"

They assume that everyone has a purpose and selfish goal when communicating. And so, they can't see honesty in my words. They are blinded by their own memories and experiences.

This stops them from finding what they are actually looking for. They may say that people lie or that everyone is trying to get something from others, but they can't see when someone doesn't do this. They can't believe it either. Their belief in how reality operates becomes their own karma. And the outcomes they get from their experiences, is indeed part of a karma that they themselves keep imposing on their own existence.

It is only the one who trusts something above himself that will put greater efforts to accept the unexpected and what seems impossible, and in doing so, change himself rapidly.

That requires a surrendering of the mind and spirit to the highest life goals. But it will also favor the greatest of all possible transformations.

When people worship a God, they tend to forget this same type of worship once they leave the temple. In other words, they focus too much on God and neglect his manifestations in daily life. And yet, that faith needs to be present in every interaction and decision to be made.

This doesn't mean that one needs to be naive and neglect the dangers that we are faced with, but rather that, once our decisions are made in wisdom, we must trust there is always a divine purpose supporting us, even in our mistakes.

You need to, to a great extent, face your fears with faith and surrender the outcomes of your decisions to a higher power — a more fulfilling purpose.

You see, many times people are receiving help when they think they are helping someone, and being taught when they think they are teaching. Only arrogance blinds them. And for many spiritual people, arrogance is the thickest blindfold they have, stopping them from getting the things they pray for.

When we understand that this state of being grants us more and faster results, we will naturally be happier, because happiness is, in essence, the idea that one is in control of his own destiny.

Chapter 13: How to Overcome Your Psychological Weaknesses?

One thing that you can noice, when spending enough time in different countries, is that you keep attracting similar experiences, and similar personalities.

That is the best indicator of the type of reality you are creating, and the best way to help you analyze it.

When we change environment, we do bring the same beliefs and thoughts with us. And that is the reason why we attract a similar reality wherever we go.

The only way to change these patterns, consists in looking into your thoughts, not towards only analyzing them but fundamentally overcoming them. That requires clarity, new insights and new perspectives, and all of these things are acquired more easily through meditation.

Exposure to the light of consciousness can be painful, but the pain felt is only an illusory and temporary challenge, because nothing hurts us more than our own ignorance.

We are often blessed by opportunities that we fail to see due to our own preconceptions, egotism and stereotypes. For this reason, whatever leads you to be more aware, either it is humiliation, failure or regret, has certainly made you more capable of reaching success.

If you don't waste time with self-pity, self-abasement, and regret, you are more likely to realize this.

Therefore, your shouldn't neglect your potential just because of what occurred in your past. Even our greatest enemies make us stronger. They teach us important lessons too, even though that is not in their intention. They teach us, for example, about the importance of solitude, self-love and self-respect.

On the other hand, the reason why so many people commit suicide these days, and can't overcome their mental struggles, is because society has made them look as their identity as a product of it. And it is very hard to overcome problems when you see yourself as part of the problem.

In many therapeutical offices, this is one of the greatest atrocities being committed, and leading patients to a worse mental state, despite any delusional perception.

You see, as soon as a person shifts her attention, — from the analysis of her choices to her personality — she has no way of winning the inner conflict occurring.

The therapist will then come out as the victorious one, the master of the personal will, but only because a vast majority is imbecile enough to consider the breaking of the personality of an individual as a person achievement.

Most of them have been broken themselves, and now overcome this sense of inferiority by breaking others in the name of help. And they may believe that they are indeed helping another person, but you never help anyone by making her believe that she is a victim of society, even when you portray yourself as being on her side.

You do more for another human being, and for yourself, when you learn how to make independent decisions that are congruent with your sense of self-worth.

Chapter 14: Why You Must Prioritize Self-Respect Over Love?

In a world lacking love, people will hurt one another more, and bully each other psychologically, to overcome their own sense of inferiority and their fears of the fellow man. But in such a world, self-love also becomes the predominant goal, often confused with loneliness.

You don't need to be alone to develop self-love. You merely need to acquire the capacity to distinguish yourself from others, and be proud of your uniqueness.

That is not something you can compare with narcissism.

In today's world, talking about oneself has become something so strange that many people get offended. And yet, you will only find true love through the awareness of our own core values.

Those who have distanced themselves from such perception, on the other hand, will claim that the ultimate truth doesn't exist, and everything is an illusion. They truly and arrogantly believe that, even though they are completely lost and suffering from depression, and can't see the correlation between their beliefs and results.

Truth does exist, as much as light does, and you find this truth by differentiating it from the lie, as much as you learn about the light by differentiating it from the darkness.

In fact, a life without an honest path, rooted in personal values, is a lost life. And a lost life always causes suffering.

The reason why so many people ask me about how to find their life purpose, is because they lack the mental and spiritual standards that could allow them to see this by themselves.

Many believe that they can find such standards in what is promoted by society. And, for example, although relationships and marriage do help, that is not enough when two individuals aren't mature enough.

Most people live as the result of the values and dynamics surrounding them, more than their own conscious decisions. Few dare going against the values of their family or culture. And so, maturity can't really occur unless one faces spiritual challenges that make him question his own identity and questions the values of his own environment. And that is more likely to occur in the presence of new environments and values, to which this person can attach.

Different people and different environments, will then stimulate different aspects of our personality, forcing us to make decisions in regards to the aspects we wish to maintain or not. And this is why real leaders walk alone, as the more you develop yourself towards becoming an independent soul, the more difficulties you will have in identifying yourself with any environment. Your own individuality has surpassed the possibility for attachment.

Modern societies may show us many cultural sub-dynamics, and more than just decades ago, but the people living in such systems have less freedom to be themselves without facing the risk of isolation. Their options within each group are actually more limited.

This gap increases as much as the power-structure deepens. Because, in larger systems, it is easier to control habits by preventing changes, than it is to control changes while allowing the transformation of habits.

Such type of systems end up then investing more in mental health, to counterbalance their own effects. But such practices also tend to become more vicious and destructive, because, as the gap increases between social systems and spiritual needs, the more destructive and permanent are the mental illnesses from which people suffer.

As Friedrich Nietzsche said, "the full extension of knowledge arises from making the unconscious conscious". Therefore, the opposite has to occur, to suppress the potential to change any system. And naturally, the more vulnerable a system is, the more this is likely to occur.

In practical terms, what I am saying here is that, as our cities keep growing, more and more people, will face the fear of discrimination, while seeing the complexity of their thinking structure being reduced.

The brightest and healthier humans will more likely be found in small cities and villages.

Already, in many cases, people are so immersed in the system that controls them, that they will protect it and attack those who challenge its values, even if the values are contrary to what one should wish for his own well-being.

That is easily noticeable in the biggest Chinese cities.

Chapter 15: The 7 Levels of Consciousness

There are seven levels to awareness or consciousness, and they are correlated with the levels of personal desire.

In each level, people perceive reality in a different way and think in different ways too, which leads them to experiences that can only be understood by those in that same level of consciousness.

Although we could label each level in different ways, they basically differentiate themselves in how narcissistic or altruistic someone has become, how brave or coward that person is in chasing her own dreams, and how consistent this person is in regards to what she says.

If we had to give names to each level, we would call them:

- Apathy, or a complete disregard for basic needs;

- Anger, and hatred towards others;

- Naiveness, or the need to defend the known world;

- Interest in changing, and a overall curiosity for information;

- Rebellious actions based on the perception of common good;

- Strong moral values rooted in profound personal experiences

- Peace of mind, or the sense of an ideal balance between the awareness of one's own potentials and limitations.

The last stage is claimed by many but accessible only to very few.

You need to feel accomplished in life, both financially and emotionally, to claim this stage for yourself.

To say that poverty is normal or good, is to either lie or be stupid, which places one in the lowest level, and not the highest as it is often assumed.

I am not saying, however, that Jesus, or many other prophets like him, are stupid, but rather that people always interpret religious scripture, and translate it too, according to their own level of consciousness, and not according to what was actually said or originally written.

You can actually discriminate any religion, based on this chart, as you will find many at the lowest levels, and others at the highest.

As you can already assume, very few will be found at the highest level, because the masses are typically attracted to what resonates with their own mental state. That is why the group of the Jehovah Witnesses keeps growing. The more stupid this group becomes, the more it will grow.

It is not a statement of quality, but rather degradation, when a group claims to easily attract the masses.

The groups that can be located at the highest levels, are the Rosicrucians, the Gnostics, and many other mystical cults and communities. Because the level of discipline, commitment and complexity, is just too high for the masses to feel any genuine interest in joining them.

Scientology and Freemasonry are two of the only groups I know that, although they could be placed on the highest level, are breathing the lowest. Because, when a group is committed to grow based on the wealth it accumulates, and the level of control it can apply on its members, it will always and naturally disintegrate itself.

I find the many members of both groups too arrogant and stupid to understand the knowledge they promote. Many of them should actually be expelled for the group to maintain a certain necessary ethical level, and yet, that doesn't happen. Both groups allow crimes against its members to occur and work hard towards suppressing public knowledges about those.

The same could be said about the many pharmaceutical companies and psychiatric committees, so this is not a personalized attack, but rather an exemplification to further clarify what I am explaining here.

Chapter 16: How to Identify the Rotten Apples of Society?

People always make decisions according to their own level of consciousness, which does make them predictable, if you look at them in such a way. Because they will see only what they can see, according to their own level, and will also reject those who are more distant from such level.

A narcissist, for example, typically in a level one or two, will attack the most those at the level six and seven, and associate himself with those at the same level. Only the stupid and the selfish will admire the narcissist.

This tendency gains a predominant importance if you compare it with the divisions that occur between those who promote constructive actions and the ones who support destruction.

I was once asked why do I think Hitler had so much power, and why are there so many evil people in the world. And my answer was simple: In both cases, evil is not perceived as evil, until it clashes with personal interests.

Most human beings are hypocrites. As many experiences in psychology show, people rarely confront the status of their own group, even when they know the group is wrong. They are more likely to change their own opinion, even when such opinion causes the suffering, or even death, of another human being.

The power of a group is very profound in the human mind, and that's why terms like "popular", "trendy" and "famous", have such an impact on people. Many of their decisions are based on these three things, rather than virtue, quality or moral.

This vast majority, living in the lowest levels of consciousness, and basically, sleep walking through life, are the ones who would die for a flag, but will do little if anything for a fellow human being.

They are the rotten apples you must avoid. Therefore, it is wiser to focus on the "good apples" among the "rotten ones", as they are much fewer and harder to find.

Many scientific experiences have shown that musicians have more areas of their brain activated and for longer periods of time, so it is not surprising that you will find a greater proportion of compassionate human beings among musicians.

If education was truly interested in creating intelligent and wise humans being, more compassionate than their ancestors, more willing to cooperate towards a common goal, more loving and open-minded, it would promote music at all levels, any type of music.

It is actually only natural that, as one goes upwards in his level of consciousness, he also develops a stronger interest for music, and not just one genre but all. This person becomes more interested in sounds and emotions than categories.

The same applies to his world views. People at the highest levels don't look at nationalities, borders, colors of skin, or even personality traits. They see everyone equally. Although they will also become more sensitive to the vibrations of their environment, which leads them to naturally prioritize kindness and generosity over any other traits.

If you want to easily identify who is at the highest spiritual level, look for those who appreciate kindness the most.

Let me give you a very simple example: Imagine that you meet a friend that is struggling in life with a problem. He describes in detail what problems he has.

Then, you go to the nearest bookstore, and buy him a book to help him solve that same problem.

Here is how he will react, according to each of the seven stages of awareness:

- If he is in apathy, he will grab the book and put in in a shelf, without saying any word to you, and he will never read that book either. This is, as you know, where the vast portion of society it;

- If your friend is angry at the world, he will complain that you shouldn't have wasted your money on a book that is most likely useless, and won't even open it either;

- If he is naive, he will read a few pages, not understand it, and put it down without finishing it.

How many people do you think you have excluded already from this simple exercise?

More than 90% for sure. But let's continue:

- if your friend is interested in changing himself, and his life, and truly wants to become a better person, he will read the whole book, and apply it;

- If your friend is rebellious, he will not only read the whole book, but also offer you one that he thinks you must read;

- If your friend has strong moral values, he will say "thank you" more than once, and then develop more compassion for you as a person;

- If your friend is in the highest level, he may not read the book, because he already possesses the knowledge, but will offer it to someone else that needs it more than he does, and will, nonetheless, accept the book, and say thank you, because he doesn't want to offend you after this generous act, and takes pride in your compassion.

Chapter 17: What to Expect From the Higher Stages of Consciousness?

The acceptance of new paradigms, is a sign of an inner transformation occurring, but also implies a revolution of the soul, as the truth transforms the mind towards deeper levels of understanding of reality, and those transpose the systems we are used to know and live with.

It's for this reason that we see more cases of depression in people with more knowledge, and especially, if they are not living according to what they know. That psychological dissonance is the cause for their depression.

Upon the acquisition of truthful and more elevated knowledge, our thinking patterns are rebuilt in order to allow for the assimilation of higher stages of complexity. And yet, for that to occur, we necessarily need to confront our former beliefs with new ones, which may cause an inner conflict, and a questioning of our own identity.

That is why, the more capable one is in confronting different realities, the wiser one will become.

The potential for knowledge, or intelligence — in its fundamental aspect — can thus be measured by the potential for confrontation, which means that an individual knows as much as what he doesn't fear knowing.

Fear is the greatest enemy of knowledge. Fearing, whatever it is, decreases the potential for wisdom in any person. Consciousness only expands due to the absence of fear, as much as fear decreases with the potential for understanding, which is acquired with knowledge and its empirical use.

You can see this principle being applied around you. That's how governments keep people under control.

The idealization of a ratio between inflation and deflation, is how governments keep their population afraid enough of losing their house and not having what to eat, but not so afraid that they will protest in mass and overthrown those in power.

In the business industry the same is applied, to manipulate people between the fear of missing out or not being socially accepted, and the need of what is being solve to them, either it is a car, clothes, or simply medicine.

The large majority of the drugs in the market, for example, intend to solve diseases caused by the food that people consume. And it is not a coincidence that many pharmaceutical corporations own both sides — the food industry and the drug industry.

These same companies then control the associations created to protect consumers, so that there is no protection stopping them from increasing their profits, but only the illusion of such, to keep people in the dark, and buying what makes them sick and keeps them sick.

As a matter of fact, medicine has always evolved towards profiting, rather than curing disease. No cure that can't be commercialized can be accepted. That is why the term "there is no cure" has become so popular.

Many want to believe that such hypocrisy is always corporative, but corporations are living organisms, embodied by real people. Many of such people, on their own, behave in the same way.

Many studies made on the dentistry, for example, have found that doctors systematically overcharge their patients and recommend procedures that they don't need.

As the bible says, "the love of money is a root of all kinds of evils" (Timothy 6:10).

There is nothing wrong with money or with wanting money. But when you "fall in love" with it, and prioritize it over moral, ethics, truth, and even human lives, that's when you are really going downwards as a human being.

Most humans, due to their tendency for egotism and hypocrisy, easily fall for this sickness of falling in love with money.

Few are those who develop a passion for activities that can only help mankind. In fact, the reason why many artists can't make a living with their art, has more to do with themselves, than art.

You see, most artists do art because they like it, and not because they care about what others want. They then anxiously try to sell what they produce, and don't understand why most people will not want it.

Their inherit predisposition to believe they are entitled to recognition is another problem, often of a mental nature.

Many times I meet writers who tell me: "I can't sell books and I don't know why".

I wonder why they think I do sell and so many.

Many of them believe I have a secret to sell so many books. They think that when I talk about value, I am overestimating myself, and reflecting their own sense of entitlement.

They really have no clue about what value is. Most artists, and not just writer, have no clue whatsoever. They may even get angry with conversations about money. It is as if many of them hated the people to whom they want to sell.

As you go upwards on the scale of consciousness, you will see that most artists are not in very high levels but low levels. And interestingly, their art will also reflect that.

Once you move to higher stages of consciousness, that is also reflected on what you do. It becomes much better.

Chapter 18: How to Identify Truthful Knowledge?

In the existential dynamic of reality, there are positive and negative forces in continuous expansion. We can talk about good and evil, but to do so, we will have to incorporate both energies at all levels, from the highest, to the lowest, from the most ethereal to the most material.

We can differentiate both forces by the fact that what is positive operates at the level of consciousness and truth, through the awareness of the soul before its existence in the spiritual realm, and its manifestation in the limited and physical spectrum of reality.

This type of awareness reaches its highest point in the dream and its subsequent experimentation as a means for transformation of personal emotions, the personality and, ultimately, if the faith is strong enough, reality itself.

The highest level of negativity is found in the most dense experimentations, such as when we feel pain, despair and the need to attack something or someone. It is at this point that chaos may assume such an unbearable state that self-destruction appears to be the only way out.

Most of the addictions of the world represent forms of escaping suffering, which is attracted through chaotic emotions and thoughts.

When someone then develops pleasure for self-destructive habits, this person is already reaching the end of the line, as not only is her life chaotic, but she is escaping it with self-destruction through pleasure, the so called coping mechanisms, rather than a higher awareness.

Naturally, we can say that the large majority of the human beings aren't really awake, but zombified by an oscillation between their suffering and their drugs or addictions. They are not centered in themselves, their true nature, but escaping it.

Here, darkness and negativity become a normal state of being. And that's why many of them ridicule religion and spirituality. They find in such behavior a justification for their situation.

It is actually interesting that people tend to attack that which they need the most, as if doing that could help them in feeling better with their misery. It is, nonetheless, a way of projecting their self-hatred.

In all the cases in which I saw hatred towards, religion, the conversation clearly indicated that such hatred appeared out of disappointment and frustration.

What is even more interesting, is that such individuals develop a certain panic for conversations on spirituality, as if afraid to get their weaknesses exposed, and betrayed again.

Coincidentally, they develop a certain paranoia around the topic of help too, which permeated the entirety of their social interactions.

I once met a woman who was always criticizing religion and claiming to be an atheist. And that didn't bother me, so I never asked why. However, I noticed that whenever I explained something that she seemed to need to understand, she would react arrogantly and become insulting.

She often answered "I already know that" or, "that is common sense".

Whatever I said to her, and even if she quite obviously didn't know already, would be attacked.

When I asked her why she was pretending to know about things that she didn't know, she denied such behavior. Maybe she couldn't even see herself suppressing any attempt at helping her in anything.

I then decided to take a different approach, to see if she was being honest or insane. I sent her a simple question in writing: "Is there something you don't know?"

She read the message, but I never got any reply. In fact, from that day onwards, she never spoke to me again.

The shocking thing about this story, is that she is a doctor.

How can we trust doctors who don't trust help? Or, in other words, how can we trust those who can't trust themselves?

Society is full of such individuals. They go through life not really living it. As when we try to operate a computer with broken pieces, or a virus in the background, sabotaging whatever we do, and erasing files, such individuals, make conversations quite complicated, and they also make us feel bad about ourselves, when in fact, the real problem is that they are deeply insane.

Chapter 19: Why is Society Disintegrating by Default?

It doesn't take much to transform the entire planet upside down, because most people have no values and no sense of moral behavior. Any form of chaos within their routines, can cause them to spin downwards and finish. The loss of a job or marriage even causes many to commit suicide, betrayals can lead to murder, and a common insult can lead to extreme forms of violence.

We have learned to tolerate the world in which we live but this world didn't change much over the past centuries. This is why the topic of carrying weapons is so debatable. You want to take weapons from society, knowing that most people are insane enough to kill, but at the same time, you know that people need weapons to protect themselves from themselves.

The solution here comes in the form of regulations and education.

Nobody seems to speak about those things, because nobody is interested on those things.

Historically speaking, however, this is not a new topic. Governments always sought to remove weapons from the population, either it was firearms or riffles or swords, to control them better.

The same was done with martial arts and even literature. In many countries, to have a concealed stick or any other martial arts weapon, is a crime. And yet, you can't stop people from using kitchen knifes, the most common weapon in robberies and crimes.

As for education, it is highly regulated, in order to avoid the formation of independent thinkers and revolutionaries, up to a point in which we can question if we are really educating or indoctrinating.

Most governments are so afraid of their people, that they remove any sense of education from education itself.

When you have so many billions of people forming their identity based on fears, slander, intrigue and conflict, you have a whole planet of humans degenerating as such.

Such people then channel their fears through the development of coping mechanisms, as the development of defensive behaviors, that are nothing more than neurotic reactions to an environment constantly perceived as threatening.

It is like living in the jungle, but not being able to identify the dangerous animals, because all animals look the same and like us — human.

Once you develop the ability to live in such circumstances, you have lost what makes you a human being. Your identity is now based on a predatory mindset.

Such individuals — narcissistic, psychopathic, neurotic, etc — may then get a sense of empowerment for being able to identify evil, but only because they are evil themselves.

You will always become that which you identify and reflect.

If you do not wish to become it, you should not need to reflect it.

You see, when I was young, I was kind and tolerant. But my parents were both imbecile and poor, so they made me grow up in one of the most violent cities in the world.

As such, I was bullied almost every day, threatened with knives and guns, and many times faced dead threats.

After much abuse, I had nothing to lose; I had no more dignity, self-respect, or even the fear of dying. But I was indeed fed up of having to deal with the same problems for so many years. And that's when I decided to train martial arts. Not one, by many.

Eventually, nobody wanted to fight me anymore. All my bullies vanished. And I too changed city, then country, over and over, again.

Then, I lost interest in the martial arts, because there was no reason to practice them. Now, when someone insults me, I ignore. I know I can fight anyone, but I am just not in the mood for that anymore.

I went back to my real self. The traumas I faced were not necessary. They did nothing for me. The world will always be hostile and dangerous. I can't fight every single person that insults me or wants to kill me. I have to move on with my life.

However, nearly all the people I met when growing up, are still there, in that cycle, disintegrating themselves. The few that moved on, carried the traumas with them, and still live in fear of the shadows of the past.

I would have never become a successful writer if I had allowed that past shape me.

Chapter 20: Why You Are What You Do?

When you complain too much about the same thing, or allow your fears to continue inside of you, not only do you attract the same more often to your life, but you also tend to attract different experiences related to it.

For example, you may not like certain behaviors in people and then find yourself one day doing the same to others.

The universe has its way of showing you the same from many angles, including your one viewpoint. Because you need to learn to overcome any negative emotion with intelligence and understanding. You can't just suppress negative emotions as many people do. That's not how we evolve.

If we could easily learn without the memories of our ancestors, there would be no books. Books exist to help us understand reality, ourselves and others, and overcome common problems.

In cultures where you had no books, you had storytellers or shamans. And they assumed the same level of importance to their tribe. Without them, every generation would simply have to restart the same stages of learning, finding themselves in continuous cycles as a group.

In today's so called civilized societies, for example, if history was explained to students, not as isolated events in the past, but karmic cycles that repeat themselves, they could learn much more and contribute more to society with such knowledge.

Reincarnation is another topic that few understand but takes a particular importance to help us look into the past.

It is due to the memories of my reincarnations that I was able to recover abilities that I had developed in previous lives. It wouldn't make any sense to be a famous author or musician by looking at my path in this life alone. I was not give anything to make it happen. On the contrary, I was often dissuaded from it, with various insults to my personality.

Many of the most famous personalities in human history, are more complex than it may seem at first sight. We are mesmerized with their achievements because we don't consider who were their mentors, which lives they had before, and so on.

Alexander the Great, for example, would not be so great without Aristotle, who was his mentor. Aristotle, on the other hand, was part of the lineage of Pythagoras, a believer in reincarnation, numerology, and student of sacred geometry.

In other words, Alexander the Great, was educated not only in philosophy, but many other arts, most of which of a very mystic nature. His greatness was traversal to him.

However, you don't just acquire such knowledge easily, unless you have been prepared before, in a previous life. So, it's not absurd to assume that he may have been a philosopher in one life, before turning into a warrior king in another.

When we look at past lives, we need to pay attention to skills, rather than social status.

When I talk about my past lives, people tend to become too obsessed with what I represented to society. But that's not relevant. It's more relevant what I learned, the type of skills acquired, and how they made me who I am today.

I have a very low tolerance for imbecility, for example, because I have been a noble and a powerful influencer of kingdoms in too many lives. But I also helped many people become rich precisely because of that background experience. My work and business strategy is much more sophisticated and vast than what most people have.

Chapter 21: Where Does Wisdom Come From?

Apart from the information we acquire in one life, or many others, there are also those among us who are often inspired by a higher power to leverage humanity to a higher ground.

Other sources of knowledge is in the people you encounter. It is a difficult task to make friends with your enemies, but necessary if you wish to understand them.

It is very difficult, for example, to understand evil without meeting evil people who can explain to you what made them evil.

The best insights I ever got on narcissism came from other narcissists. And it's very interesting when two people who never met in person, know more about each other than I do about any of them, and despite knowing both in person for many years. And this, just because they are narcissists and I am not.

They both can't understand my way of thinking and decisions in life, but both understand each other perfectly well, without ever seeing one another.

That is very impressive, but has to do with the vibrations in which different personalities are. As mentioned before, in every stage of life, we will attract similar patterns in our environment.

This could lead us to easily conclude that narcissists would be able to love each other more easily than other people but, ironically, such isn't the case. Narcissists fall in love with other narcissists but can't really accept their behaviors. They always seek the ones they envy the most, and want to destroy — people who are successful, happy, and kind.

Now, this would lead us to think that, at least, they could change themselves upon realizing that they can't handle the ones who reflect their own behaviors. But that doesn't happen. And that's why Narcissism is a mental disorder — The Narcissist sees himself, rejects himself, but refuses to change.

Narcissists keep increasing that dark inner world and, quite literally, running from their own shadow at the same time. That is also why they become worse over the years.

One of my former girlfriends, who is a narcissist, for example, went from posting photos with me, smiling, to know make evil horns in her hand in nearly all the photos she takes, as if she was proud to be evil, and needed to state that openly.

Another thing that I find interesting is how the people around her behave. Because you see them in some photos being hugged by her, smiling, and then months later, you see them in the corner of the photo, with a face like they have met the devil in person.

The problem with narcissism is exactly that. The narcissist doesn't realize that she is mentally sick, so she suppresses the sickness with pride, in a twisted version of reality.

Instead of thinking, "I am an idiot and I lose friends all the time", the narcissist thinks "I have a strong personality and men are cowards";

Instead of looking at herself in the mirror and saying, "

You can understand narcissism by twisting everything that is bad into a personal quality, because that's what narcissists do in their head. They are too stupid to realize who they are, but much smarter than the rest of us, in the art of manipulation. Because, due precisely to their nature, and fears, they become extremely good at analyzing the weaknesses in others and their vulnerabilities, in order to manipulate them and abuse them.

The narcissist is very skillful in manipulating anyone, as I have seen, including those you would assume to be too smart to be manipulated by anyone. They have different strategies for everyone, and they don't mind spending hours learning how to control such people.

One narcissist I knew, for example, would study the cultural dating habits of all the men she encountered. Before they even thought about seducing her, she was already manipulating them.

Another one, would explore the sexual needs of others in seemly innocent conversations, as a way to gain their trust. Because, after all, if you expose your vulnerabilities at such as deep level with someone, you then also feel naturally vulnerable in her presence.

In another case, she would use victimization and pity, to gain the support of others. And if that did not work, she would create the circumstances that would allow her to gather evidences, such as provoking me with her mobile in hands, in order to record my reactions. The abuse would then continue and become more vicious, in order to gather as much evidence as possible on her side.

What is interesting about this last story in particular, is that she was gathering evidence to prove to her family, that their daughter, who they know since birth, is not crazy, and her boyfriend, whom they met for only a couple of days, and was a polite and hardworking author and business owner, is the crazy one.

I used to say to her: "I have been in religious groups all my life, and you think I am the evil one?"

Her answer would always be: "You pretend not to be evil, but you are".

You see, narcissists live in a very twisted reality. It's a waste of time to argue logic with them. But what makes them particularly interesting, as a subspecies, is that they expose how imbecile and controllable the rest of society is.

You can learn a lot about narcissistic behavior, but never as much as you will near about yourself and others in relation to such behaviors.

It was thanks to the narcissists I met, that I learned about the wounds I have within me, stopping me from reaching my maximum potential as a human being.

That narcissist I met were very good at finding and then using my own past traumas against me, and that forced me to eliminate them by direct confrontation with myself.

If it was not for our enemies, we would never have a chance at discovering our greatest weaknesses.

Chapter 22: Why are Narcissists Our Greatest Teachers?

Some of the things that became obvious to me from my analysis of the narcissists, was that, the lower the spiritual level of a person, the more this person will focus on personal gains and make decisions based on fear, never really making an analysis of reality that considers commitments or the common well-being.

In other words, due to their own fears, they betray others, and in doing so, justify those same fears, such as the fear of abandonment.

It is actually sad to realize how far they will play this game, as when a narcissist woman tries to pull me back to a relationship after admitting to have cheated.

That's abuse at the ultimate level. You betray the other person in any way and form you will, and then try to get that person back, as if it was some game, and are even surprised that this same person chooses to abandon you instead.

I am sure this is what they tell others: "He abandoned me."

I also realized that they play this game so profoundly, and in such as repetitive form, in order to escape shame — another of their fears — that they end up forgetting the facts and confusing the reality they know, as if the lie became more real than what they experienced.

I noticed that most narcissists live at a very psychotic level, meaning that they repeat their lies so often to others, that they end up believing them in their head.

That cognitive dissonance becomes too difficult to handle, because they need to deny at all costs that they are the crazy ones.

Again, this is mental illness. The person is purposely distorting facts in order to avoid blame and responsibility, and in doing so, escapes her own consciousness and denies herself an opportunity to learn from her own mistakes.

As a result, the narcissist repeats the same pattern with every single person they encounter.

Most of the evil in this world, is done out of ignorance and fear, and this is why such individuals fail to recognize the impact of their actions on themselves, always shifting responsibility to someone else that they choose to blame.

The desperation of someone who decides to rob a bank and spend the rest of his life in prison, for example, is, to a great extent, the result of an individual who didn't believe in himself enough to start a business, didn't develop the necessary skills to get a proper job, and was too stupid to see any alternatives once he reached what is called "point of no return".

Here, the no return point is the overwhelming need for immediate payments.

Desperation is always the result of insufficient preparation, unwise decisions and naive world views.

The lower the spiritual state of such individuals, the harder it is for them to actually recognize happiness, reason why they tend to associate themselves with those who have a similar nature, and will deviate them from the ideal path.

The people you associate yourself with will either increase your potential to achieve what you always wanted or make you doubt yourself and your decisions for long enough to fail drastically.

When you listen to the self-destructive logics based on selfishness and envy, and to the suggestions that seem to reinforce your own selfish desires, you increase your potential for failure. And yet, there is nothing a narcissist like to hear the most when complaining about a partner than the words "you deserve better", as it justifies their betrayals.

The phrase 'you deserve better' has a contradictory meaning, depending on who says it. It is either directed at preying on your pride to manipulate you, or save you from your own mistakes.

As a matter of fact, the narcissist mind can't feel love or empathy but only pride, which shows us that pride is the lowest state of the mind and love the highest, and both can't be associated in the same level of perceptions.

On the other hand, pride is fundamentally a distortion of self-esteem. Pride is a replacement for the inability to self-love. By making her decisions based on pride, the narcissist sabotages her own results and becomes easily deceived, and ironically, by other narcissists.

The only way anyone is able to save herself from deception rooted on pride, is by separating herself from her egotistical needs.

That demands a shift of attention from the social masks one builds to interact with others, and towards the real and spiritual self.

That tasks shows itself very difficult because we are often pressured by those we care the most into fulfilling their expectations or risk losing them forever. And because humans are fundamentally emotional creatures, the need for happiness always requires a certain dose of psychopathy.

You have to prioritize yourself enough to achieve your results, or you may never do, if what you seek contradicts the world views of those who surround you.

It's at this moment that there is a crucial difference between all human beings showing itself, and essentially between those who follow the path of social acceptance or accept rejection and isolation naturally, because the first are sheep and the second leaders. There is not in-between state unless, as mentioned, you are lucky enough to have your own views matching the views of others.

Only in the latter case does it become possible to discuss the topic of transformation of the personality.

In the first situation, it doesn't matter how many therapists a person sees or books she reads, as the progress will be too insignificant to be considered.

Nonetheless, much of what in psychology and psychiatry tends to be diagnosed as personality disorder, is actually a social discrimination of all individuals who opt for their spirituality rather than the social constructs, and end up discovering aspects that transform them in unacceptable ways to many.

The debate among many psychologists and psychiatrists on what should be labeled as an illness or not, tends to actually be directed also on what should be considered socially acceptable or not.

In a way, psychiatrists do determine the path in which the world should go.

Chapter 23: What is the Correlation Between Reincarnation and Mental Health?

The most indisputable path for mental health is also the most avoided, because it would nullify much of what is believed today.

Sadly, this field is also filled more with speculation than truths. These truths would have to be scientific and science doesn't dare to go there yet. I am referring to reincarnation.

It is impossible to talk about spirituality without referring past lives, because, as soon as you start to awake, this topic becomes self-evident, and not another issue determined by opinions or common logic.

In fact, the more you awaken memories from other lives, the more competent you become in different areas, the more complex your identity is, and the faster you are in determining your own fate.

Nearly everything that puzzles people about my personality, such as my capacity to be able in many different fields and achieve high results, how fast I change my values, and how easily I adapt to any situation, or even the amount of information contained in my books, comes from my awareness of my previous lives. And yet, people look at the evidence and refuse to accept the causes.

Really too many times, I have heard, "that is not possible", or "nobody has so much knowledge", or even "it's impossible for anyone to know so much"; as if who I am wasn't real. And yet, here I am, proving everything I say to them, and hearing them reject the evidences.

It is very challenging when people literally tell you that you don't exist.

I believe, that is the ultimate challenge to our identity as a spirit. And if it wasn't for the truth behind all this knowledge, the consequences of such rejection would leave me in a bad state psychologically.

It's hard when people refuse your own existence, your own right to be who you really are. But they do it all the time. They literally don't let you be who you are, if who you are shows an unacceptable gap between your nature and theirs.

It's actually funny that christians refer to Jesus all the time as a symbol of social rejection to the truths, because all the christians I ever met rejected me for not agreeing with them.

People live with boxes in their head. They don't see reality and they don't want to see it either. They feel safe in their little world. And they then use historical references to justify such limitations, as if Jesus ever approved such type of discrimination.

He actually represented the exact opposite, by accepting all types of people around him. And that's what got him killed — unconditional love.

I never met a christian with unconditional love, so I can't say I ever met a real christian.

Christianity, as many other religions, and science too, would be challenged if we really looked at them as what they are — perspectives of the same truth. And this would, again, lead us to accept reincarnation as part of all.

Once you start awaking for the possibility of possessing many perspectives showing the same reality, you also come to the realization that the idea of personality makes very little sense, especially when you confront your own newly acquired capacity to flow through many personalities adopted over hundreds, thousands or even millions of years.

Once you see yourself as an immortal spirit occupying many bodies and having many life experiences, identifying yourself as who you are now, defending a nationality, or being racist, or xenophobic, becomes ridiculous.

As a matter of fact, the most xenophobic and nationalistic people I ever met are also, and not coincidentally, the most imbecile. They don't really understand what makes human beings human. And they are often cruel in their social interactions too.

The more imbecile a person is, the more offensive this person becomes to anything that challenges her status quo.

Chapter 24: What the Personality is from a Spiritual Viewpoint?

One cannot speak of a personality with many previous lives, but instead multiple personalities in a unique spiritual line of existence.

This can seem confusing from a psychological point of view, reason why psychology typically avoids the topic as a whole.

You need to really debate and rethink a lot of the most well-accepted mental disorders to determine what becomes one or not in a spiritually awaken person. Because, this person, should actually fit the criteria of mentally healthy, if his spiritual path has been followed correctly.

By followed correctly, I mean organically, according to the rules of nature and the cosmos, most of which has been properly described by many mystics throughout time, from India to Egypt and many other former civilizations that have already perished, and can only be found at the bottom of the ocean, and even though such huge cities are abundant all over the planet.

There wasn't only one Atlantis but many. Although we can debate if Atlantis was, in particular, a more advanced society, it is now, from an archeological point of view, indisputable, that Egypt wasn't the most advanced civilization in our past, or even Babylon.

There was much more wisdom and knowledge before that, and much more complex societies too. Most of which were likely rules by extraterrestrial beings. It is thanks to them that the first world maps appear.

It is actually interesting that the Portuguese and Spaniards claim to have discovered the routes to much of was not yet know as new parts of the world, while the truth is that both countries were founded and funded by the Knights Templar, an organization that was much more interested in the development of medieval Europe, due to their association to all the kingdoms, than they were to christianity in particular, which seemed like a very small and limiting approach to the spiritual truth they became in contact with through their friends in the middle east.

Once the maps of the entire globe came to their hands, it was only a matter of time to discover how to get there. In other words, they already knew how the world looked like. They just didn't know how to get to different part by sea.

We can compare that to the situation of the internet today. Because, you see, the internet comes from this idea, also know for many centuries, that we can communicate through non-physical means, merely using frequency, and vibration.

It is not a far reach of imagination to consider that we are literally withdrawing information and physical content from the air, when we download videos and music.

Our 3D printers can now do this using chemicals. But it will come a time in which what they will be able to do, will seem like magic, as they will not need the chemicals within them, but will also withdraw such chemicals from the environment, much like what we do when processing air into water.

This alchemical process has always fascinated mystics, because it's the foundation of our spiritual transmutation, as well as the transmutation of the world. Is the language of God.

In regards to this topic, I find it interesting to compare the type of people who constantly insult me with those who admire me. Because the only type of people who admire me are business owners, freemasons and rosicrucians.

Those who ridicule me are the peasants of medieval times, although now, they keep the same mindset even though having college degrees, a desk and a computer to work.

Many, truly many, of the most stupid people I ever met, seem perfectly normal to the rest of society.

The business owners I encountered, on the other hand, many times added insights to my lifestyle that I never considered before, and yet, are true.

One of them said that I make money from the sky. And he said it as if it was some form of magic.

He was right. I take the information from the non-visible reality, and transform it into physical things, such as books, with value, that will then sell, and bring to me the money I need to travel, pay for housing and food, and buy objects that help me with my work.

I literally use magic to create my lifestyle. And that is why, for the rest of the population, I seem scary, confusing, and secretive.

One person recently said I am very mysterious. And yes, that may seem too. But i am only mysterious to the dumb, as I write everything I know.

What is truly mysterious is human imbecility, because if someone like me is sharing everything he knows, the real mystery is: Why isn't everyone reading?

If more people read my books, our planet would advance much more rapidly, and those 3D printers I mentioned before, would probably be a reality already.

The interesting thing about magic is that, like spirituality, is merely a tool to help us reach our full potential. It is not something outside of us, but something within us.

It is sad, when, for religious reasons, people get scared of magic. Because, when that happens, not only do they limit their own potential, and the potential of society, but also make themselves vulnerable to ignorance.

Many christians don't understand that, although magic opens the doors to the occult, from which demons may come, the lack of it, doesn't make demons disappear. Many christians, that go to church every Sunday, and pray every day, are themselves possessed. And the only reason why I know this is because I know enough about magic to see it in its most hidden forms.

"The greatest trick the Devil ever pulled was convincing the world he didn't exist" (Charles Baudelaire). "The second greatest trick the Devil ever pulled was convincing the world he is the good guy" (Ken Ammi).

About the Publisher

This book was published by the 22 Lions Bookstore.
 For more books like this visit www.22Lions.com.
 Join us on social media at:
 Fb.com/22Lions;
 Twitter.com/22lionsbookshop;
 Instagram.com/22lionsbookshop;
 Pinterest.com/22LionsBookshop.

www.ingramcontent.com/pod-product-compliance
Lightning Source LLC
Chambersburg PA
CBHW071910070526
44583CB00016B/1930